pocket posh®
100 classic love poems

Edited by Jennifer Fox

Andrews McMeel
Publishing, LLC

Kansas City · Sydney · London

POCKET POSH® 100 CLASSIC LOVE POEMS

copyright © 2012 by Andrews McMeel Publishing, LLC. All rights reserved. Printed in China. No part of this book may be used or reproduced in any manner whatsoever without written permission except in the case of reprints in the context of reviews.

Andrews McMeel Publishing, LLC
an Andrews McMeel Universal company
1130 Walnut Street, Kansas City, Missouri 64106

www.andrewsmcmeel.com

12 13 14 15 16 SHZ 10 9 8 7 6 5 4 3 2 1

ISBN: 978-1-4494-2162-5

Library of Congress Control Number: 2012935528

Illustration © Lily Ashbury Design

ATTENTION: SCHOOLS AND BUSINESSES
Andrews McMeel books are available at quantity discounts with bulk purchase for educational, business, or sales promotional use. For information, please e-mail the Andrews McMeel Publishing Special Sales Department: specialsales@amuniversal.com

808.8193543 Pocket

Pocket posh 100 classic love poems

$7.99   30519009319651

introduction ix
 1 Sonnet 56   1
 2 You'll Love Me Yet (from *Pippa Passes*)   2
 3 Bequest   3
 4 Sonnet 75   4
 5 Sonnet 43   5
 6 He Wishes for the Cloths of Heaven   6
 7 Sonnet 8   7
 8 Love in Autumn   8
 9 More Strong Than Time   9
 10 A Birthday   10
 11 Sonnet 116   11
 12 I Am Shut Out of Mine Own Heart   12
 13 Love's Philosophy   13
 14 Sonnet 27   14
 15 Marriage Morning   15
 16 Excursion Train   17
 17 A Sonnet of the Moon   19
 18 To My Dear and Loving Husband   20
 19 She Was a Phantom of Delight   21
 20 Sonnet 42   22

21 She Walks in Beauty   23
22 Love   24
23 I Love You   26
24 I Have No Life but This   27
25 The Presence of Love   28
26 Song: To Celia   29
27 Bright Star   30
28 Two in the Campagna   31
29 Eros   34
30 The Owl and the Pussy-Cat   35
31 Love and Harmony   37
32 If You Were Coming in the Fall   38
33 Remember   39
34 Sonnet 154   40
35 Meet Me in the Green Glen   41
36 I Am Not Yours   42
37 All for Love   43
38 A Red, Red Rose   44
39 It's All I Have to Bring Today   45
40 Sonnet 18   46
41 Secret Love   46
42 From the Arabic: An Imitation   48
43 A Decade   49
44 Sweet-and-Twenty   50
45 Sonnet 33   51
46 Love Will Find Out the Way   52
47 The Clod and the Pebble   55
48 Love   56

49 The Definition of Love   57
50 First Love   59
51 Her Voice   61
52 Sonnet 21   63
53 Echo   64
54 Sonnet 40   65
55 The White Rose   66
56 Central Park at Dusk   66
57 Sonnet 12   67
58 Love and Death   68
59 In a Boat   69
60 Life in a Love   71
61 Sonnet 35   72
62 Wooing Song   73
63 Annabel Lee   75
64 Snow Song   77
65 Sonnet 47   78
66 Monna Innominata (I Loved You First)   79
67 Sonnet 34   80
68 Stanzas ["Oh, Come to Me in Dreams, My Love!"]   81
69 Wild Nights—Wild Nights!   82
70 The Rose and the Bee   83
71 Lovers' Infiniteness   84
72 Sonnet 14   86
73 The Indian Serenade   87
74 I Would Live in Your Love   88
75 The Letter   89
76 The Ragged Wood   90

77 Sonnet 130 91
78 When the Lamp Is Shattered 92
79 Joy 94
80 Monna Innominata [I Wish I Could Remember] 95
81 A Love Song 96
82 Spring Night 98
83 The Passionate Shepherd to His Love 99
84 Sonnet 10 101
85 Good-Night 102
86 Romance 103
87 Peace 104
88 Down by the Salley Gardens 105
89 Opal 105
90 Surrender 106
91 A Complaint 107
92 Meeting at Night 108
93 Sonnet 137 109
94 The Genesis of Butterflies 110
95 Corinne's Last Love Song 111
96 Leave Me, O Love, Which Reachest but to Dust 112
97 Sonnet 22 113
98 Music, When Soft Voices Die 114
99 Less Than the Cloud to the Wind 114
100 The Lily 115

author index 116

introduction

Love is such a simple, beautiful word. If only being in love were that easy! Instead, it is a complicated, ever-changing jumble of feelings and emotions. It can be pure and joyful and unconditional. But it can also be jealous and bitter and unforgiving. The selections I chose for this collection of classic love poetry reflect that dichotomy. From the aching hopefulness of "I Am Not Yours" by Sara Teasdale and "You'll Love Me Yet" by Robert Browning to the blissful contentment of Elizabeth Barrett Browning's "How Do I Love Thee?" and William Blake's "Love and Harmony," there is a verse that will resonate with you no matter what stage of love you are experiencing. Wherever you are in your life journey, I encourage you to allow yourself to be carried away by the passion of this eclectic collection of love poems.

1) Sonnet 56

Sweet love, renew thy force; be it not said
Thy edge should blunter be than appetite,
Which but to-day by feeding is allay'd,
To-morrow sharpen'd in his former might:
So, love, be thou; although to-day thou fill
Thy hungry eyes even till they wink with fullness,
To-morrow see again, and do not kill
The spirit of love with a perpetual dullness.
Let this sad interim like the ocean be
Which parts the shore, where two contracted new
Come daily to the banks, that, when they see
Return of love, more blest may be the view;
> Else call it winter, which being full of care
> Makes summer's welcome thrice more wish'd,
> more rare.

—*William Shakespeare*

2. You'll Love Me Yet (from *Pippa Passes*)

You'll love me yet!—and I can tarry
    Your love's protracted growing:
June reared that bunch of flowers you carry,
    From seeds of April's sowing.

I plant a heartful now: some seed
    At least is sure to strike,
And yield—what you'll not pluck indeed,
    Not love, but, may be, like.

You'll look at least on love's remains,
    A grave's one violet:
Your look?—that pays a thousand pains.
    What's death? You'll love me yet!
    —Robert Browning

3) Bequest

You left me, sweet, two legacies,—
A legacy of love
A Heavenly Father would content,
Had He the offer of;

You left me boundaries of pain
Capacious as the sea,
Between eternity and time,
Your consciousness and me.
	—*Emily Dickinson*

4) Sonnet 75

One day I wrote her name upon the strand,
    but came the waves and washed it away:
    again I wrote it with a second hand,
    but came the tide and made my pains his prey.
Vain man, said she, thou dost in vain assay
    a mortal thing so to immortalize;
    for I myself shall like to this decay,
    and eke my name be wiped out likewise.
Not so, (quod I) let baser things devise
    to die in dust, but you shall live by fame:
    my verse your virtues rare shall eternize,
    and in the heavens write your glorious name:
Where, when as Death shall all the world subdue,
    our love shall live, and later life renew.
    —*Edmund Spenser*

5) Sonnet 43

How do I love thee? Let me count the ways.
I love thee to the depth and breadth and height
My soul can reach, when feeling out of sight
For the ends of Being and ideal Grace.
I love thee to the level of every day's
Most quiet need, by sun and candlelight.
I love thee freely, as men strive for Right;
I love thee purely, as they turn from Praise.
I love thee with the passion put to use
In my old griefs, and with my childhood's faith.
I love thee with a love I seemed to lose
With my lost saints,—I love thee with the breath,
Smiles, tears, of all my life!—and, if God choose,
I shall but love thee better after death.
    —*Elizabeth Barrett Browning*

6   He Wishes for the Cloths of Heaven

Had I the heavens' embroidered cloths,
Enwrought with the golden and silver light,
The blue and the dim and the dark cloths
Of night and light and half-light,
I would spread the cloths under your feet
But I, being poor, have only my dreams;
I have spread my dreams beneath your feet;
Tread softly because you tread on my dreams.

—*William Butler Yeats*

7 Sonnet 8

Set me where as the sun doth parch the green,
Or where his beams do not dissolve the ice;
In temperate heat where he is felt and seen;
With proud people, in presence sad and wise;
Set me in base, or yet in high degree,
In the long night, or in the shortest day,
In clear weather, or where mists thickest be,
In lost youth, or when my hairs be grey;
Set me in earth, in heaven, or yet in hell,
In hill, in dale, or in the foaming flood;
Thrall, or at large, alive where so I dwell,
Sick, or in health, in ill fame or good:
Yours will I be, and with that only thought
Comfort myself when that my hope is nought.

—*Petrarch*

8 Love in Autumn

I sought among the drifting leaves,
    The golden leaves that once were green,
To see if Love were hiding there
    And peeping out between.

For thro' the silver showers of May
    And thro' the summer's heavy heat,
In vain I sought his golden head
    And light, fast-flying feet.

Perhaps when all the world is bare
    And cruel winter holds the land,
The Love that finds no place to hide
    Will run and catch my hand.

I shall not care to have him then,
    I shall be bitter and a-cold—
It grows too late for frolicking
    When all the world is old.

The little hiding Love, come forth,
    Come forth before the autumn goes,
And let us seek thro' ruined paths
    The garden's last red rose.
    —*Sara Teasdale*

9. More Strong Than Time

Since I have set my lips to your full cup, my sweet,
Since I my pallid face between your hands have laid,
Since I have known your soul, and all the bloom of it,
And all the perfume rare, now buried in the shade;

Since it was given to me to hear one happy while,
The words wherein your heart spoke all its mysteries,
Since I have seen you weep, and since I have seen you smile,
Your lips upon my lips, and your eyes upon my eyes;

Since I have known above my forehead glance and gleam,
A ray, a single ray, of your star, veiled always,
Since I have felt the fall, upon my lifetime's stream,
Of one rose petal plucked from the roses of your days;

I now am bold to say to the swift changing hours,
Pass, pass upon your way, for I grow never old,
Fleet to the dark abysm with all your fading flowers,
One rose that none may pluck, within my heart I hold.

Your flying wings may smite, but they can never spill
The cup fulfilled of love, from which my lips are wet;
My heart has far more fire than you have frost to chill,
My soul more love than you can make my soul forget.
  —*Victor Hugo*

10) A Birthday

My heart is like a singing bird
    Whose nest is in a water'd shoot;
My heart is like an apple-tree
    Whose boughs are bent with thick-set fruit;
My heart is like a rainbow shell
    That paddles in a halcyon sea;
My heart is gladder than all these,
    Because my love is come to me.

Raise me a daïs of silk and down;
    Hang it with vair and purple dyes;
Carve it in doves and pomegranates,
    And peacocks with a hundred eyes;
Work it in gold and silver grapes,
    In leaves and silver fleurs-de-lys;
Because the birthday of my life
    Is come, my love is come to me.
    —Christina Rossetti

11 Sonnet 116

Let me not to the marriage of true minds
Admit impediments. Love is not love
Which alters when it alteration finds,
Or bends with the remover to remove:
O, no! it is an ever-fixed mark
That looks on tempests and is never shaken;
It is the star to every wandering bark,
Whose worth's unknown, although his height be taken.
Love's not Time's fool, though rosy lips and cheeks
Within his bending sickle's compass come:
Love alters not with his brief hours and weeks,
But bears it out even to the edge of doom.
    If this be error and upon me proved,
    I never writ, nor no man ever loved.
  —*William Shakespeare*

I Am Shut Out of Mine Own Heart

I am shut out of mine own heart
because my Love is far from me
nor in the wonders have I part
that fills its hidden empery:

the wildwood of adventurous thought
and lands of dawn my dream had won,
the riches out of Faerie brought
are buried with our bridal sun;

and I am in a narrow place,
and all its little streets are cold,
because the absence of her face
hath reft the sullen air of gold.

My home is in a broader day:
—sometimes I catch it glistening
thro' the dull gate, a flower'd play
and odour of undying Spring:

the long days that I lived alone,
sweet madness of the Springs I miss'd,
are shed beyond, and thro' them blown
clear laughter, and my lips are kiss'd:

—and here from mine own joy apart,
I wait the turning of the key:
I am shut out of mine own heart
because my Love is far from me.
    —*Christopher John Brennan*

13 Love's Philosophy

I
The fountains mingle with the river
    And the rivers with the Ocean,
The winds of Heaven mix for ever
    With a sweet emotion;
Nothing in the world is single;
    All things by a law divine
In one another's being mingle—
    Why not I with thine?

II
See the mountains kiss high Heaven,
    And the waves clasp one another;
No sister-flower would be forgiven
    If it disdain'd its brother;
And the sunlight clasps the earth,
    And the moonbeams kiss the sea—
What are all these kissings worth,
    If thou kiss not me?
    —*Percy Bysshe Shelley*

14 Sonnet 27

My own Beloved, who hast lifted me
From this drear flat of earth where I was thrown,
And, in betwixt the languid ringlets, blown
A life-breath, till the forehead hopefully
Shines out again, as all the angels see,
Before thy saving kiss! My own, my own,
Who camest to me when the world was gone,
And I who looked for only God, found thee!
I find thee; I am safe, and strong, acid glad.
As one who stands in dewless asphodel,
Looks backward on the tedious time he had
In the upper life,—so I, with bosom-swell,
Make witness, here, between the good and bad,
That Love, as strong as Death, retrieves as well.

—*Elizabeth Barrett Browning*

15 Marriage Morning

Light, so low upon earth,
    You send a flash to the sun.
Here is the golden close of love,
    All my wooing is done.
Oh, all the woods and the meadows,
    Woods, where we hid from the wet,
Stiles where we stayed to be kind,
    Meadows in which we met!

Light, so low in the vale
    You flash and lighten afar,
For this is the golden morning of love,
    And you are his morning star.
Flash, I am coming, I come,
    By meadow and stile and wood,
Oh, lighten into my eyes and my heart,
    Into my heart and my blood!

Heart, are you great enough
    For a love that never tires?
O heart, are you great enough for love?
    I have heard of thorns and briers.
Over the thorns and briers,
    Over the meadows and stiles,
Over the world to the end of it
    Flash a million miles.
    —Alfred, Lord Tennyson

16) **Excursion Train**

I wonder, can the night go by;
Can this shot arrow of travel fly
Shaft-golden with light, sheer into the sky
    Of a dawned to-morrow,
Without ever sleep delivering us
From each other, or loosing the dolorous
    And turgid sorrow!

What is it then that you can see
That at the window endlessly
You watch the red sparks whirl and flee
    And the night look through?
Your presence peering lonelily there
Oppresses me so, I can hardly bear
    To share the train with you.

You hurt my heart-beats' privacy;
I wish I could put you away from me;
I suffocate in this intimacy,
    For all that I love you;
How I have longed for this night in the train,
Yet now every fibre of me cries in pain
    To God to remove you.

Though surely my soul's best dream is still
That one night pouring down shall swill
Us away in an utter sleep, until
    We are one, smooth-rounded.
Yet closely bitten in to me
Is this armour of stiff reluctancy
    That keeps me impounded.

So, Helen when another night
Comes on us, lift your fingers white
And strip me naked, touch me light,
    Light, light all over.
For I ache most earnestly for your touch,
Yet I cannot move, however much
    I would be your lover.

Night after night with a blemish of day
Unblown and unblossomed has withered away;
Come another night, come a new night, say
    Will you pluck me apart?
Will you open the amorous, aching bud
Of my body, and loose the burning flood
    That would pour to you from my heart?
    —D. H. Lawrence

17. A Sonnet of the Moon

Look how the pale queen of the silent night
Doth cause the ocean to attend upon her,
And he, as long as she is in his sight,
With her full tide is ready her to honor.
But when the silver waggon of the moon
Is mounted up so high he cannot follow,
The sea calls home his crystal waves to moan,
And with low ebb doth manifest his sorrow.
So you that are the sovereign of my heart
Have all my joys attending on your will;
My joys low-ebbing when you do depart,
When you return their tide my heart doth fill.
So as you come and as you do depart,
Joys ebb and flow within my tender heart.

—*Charles Best*

18 To My Dear and Loving Husband

If ever two were one then surely we.
If ever man were loved by wife, then thee;
If ever wife were happy in a man,
Compare with me, ye women, if you can.
I prize thy love more than whole mines of gold
Or all the riches that the East doth hold.
My love is such that rivers cannot quench,
Nor aught but love from thee give recompense.
Thy love is such I can no way repay;
The heavens reward thee manifold, I pray.
Then while we live, in love let's so persevere
That when we live no more, we may live ever.

   —*Anne Bradstreet*

19 She Was a Phantom of Delight

She was a Phantom of delight
When first she gleam'd upon my sight;
A lovely Apparition, sent
To be a moment's ornament;
Her eyes as stars of Twilight fair;
Like Twilight's, too, her dusky hair;
But all things else about her drawn
From May-time and the chearful Dawn;
A dancing Shape, an Image gay,
To haunt, to startle, and way-lay.
I saw her upon nearer view,
A Spirit, yet a Woman too!
Her household motions light and free,
And steps of virgin-liberty;
A countenance in which did meet
Sweet records, promises as sweet;
A Creature not too bright or good
For human nature's daily food,
For transient sorrows, simple wiles,
Praise, blame, love, kisses, tears, and smiles.
And now I see with eye serene
The very pulse of the machine;
A Being breathing thoughtful breath,
A Traveller between life and death:
The reason firm, the temperate will,

Endurance, foresight, strength, and skill;
A perfect Woman, nobly plann'd
To warn, to comfort, and command;
And yet a Spirit still, and bright
With something of angelic light.
　　—*William Wordsworth*

20 Sonnet 42

That thou hast her, it is not all my grief,
And yet it may be said I loved her dearly;
That she hath thee, is of my wailing chief,
A loss in love that touches me more nearly.
Loving offenders, thus I will excuse ye:
Thou dost love her, because thou know'st I love her;
And for my sake even so doth she abuse me,
Suffering my friend for my sake to approve her.
If I lose thee, my loss is my love's gain,
And losing her, my friend hath found that loss;
Both find each other, and I lose both twain,
And both for my sake lay on me this cross:
　　But here's the joy; my friend and I are one;
　　Sweet flattery! then she loves but me alone.
　　—*William Shakespeare*

21 She Walks in Beauty

I
She walks in beauty like the night
    Of cloudless climes and starry skies;
And all that's best of dark and bright
    Meet in her aspect and her eyes:
Thus mellowed to the tender light
    Which heaven to gaudy day denies.

II
One ray the more, one shade the less,
    Had half impair'd the nameless grace
Which waves in every raven tress
    Or softly lightens o'er her face;
Where thoughts serenely sweet express
    How pure, how dear their dwelling-place.

III
And on that cheek, and o'er that brow
    So soft, so calm, yet eloquent,
The smiles that win, the tints that glow,
    But tell of days in goodness spent,
A mind at peace with all below,
    A heart whose love is innocent!

   – –Lord Byron

22 Love

Love, though it is not chill and cold,
　　But burning like eternal fire,
Is yet not of approaches bold,
　　Which gay dramatic tastes admire.
Oh timid love, more fond than free,
　　In daring song is ill pourtrayed,
Where, as in war, the devotee
　　By valour wins each captive maid;—

Where hearts are prest to hearts in glee,
　　As they could tell each other's mind;
Where ruby lips are kissed as free,
　　As flowers are by the summer wind.
No! gentle love, that timid dream,
　　With hopes and fears at foil and play,
Works like a skiff against the stream,
　　And thinking most finds least to say.

It lives in blushes and in sighs,
    In hopes for which no words are found;
Thoughts dare not speak but in the eyes,
    The tongue is left without a sound.
The pert and forward things that dare
    Their talk in every maiden's ear,
Feel no more than their shadows there—
    Mere things of form, with nought of fear.

True passion, that so burns to plead,
    Is timid as the dove's disguise;
'Tis for the murder-aiming gleed
    To dart at every thing that flies.
True love, it is no daring bird,
    But like the little timid wren,
That in the new-leaved thorns of spring
    Shrinks farther from the sight of men.

The idol of his musing mind,
    The worship of his lonely hour,
Love woos her in the summer wind,
    And tells her name to every flower;
But in her sight, no open word
    Escapes, his fondness to declare;
The sighs by beauty's magic stirred
    Are all that speak his passion there.
    —*John Clare*

23) I Love You

When April bends above me
    And finds me fast asleep,
Dust need not keep the secret
    A live heart died to keep.

When April tells the thrushes,
    The meadow-larks will know,
And pipe the three words lightly
    To all the winds that blow.

Above his roof the swallows,
    In notes like far-blown rain,
Will tell the little sparrow
    Beside his window-pane.

O sparrow, little sparrow,
    When I am fast asleep,
Then tell my love the secret
    That I have died to keep.

—*Sara Teasdale*

I Have No Life but This

I have no Life but this—
To lead it here—
Nor any Death—but lest
Dispelled from there—

Nor tie to Earths to come—
Nor Action new—
Except through this extent—
The Realm of you—
    —*Emily Dickinson*

25 The Presence of Love

              And in Life's noisiest hour,
There whispers still the ceaseless Love of Thee,
           The heart's Self-solace and soliloquy.

You mould my Hopes, you fashion me within;
    And to the leading Love-throb in the Heart
        Thro' all my Being, thro' my pulse's beat;
You lie in all my many Thoughts, like Light,
Like the fair light of Dawn, or summer Eve
On rippling Stream, or cloud-reflecting Lake.
And looking to the Heaven, that bends above you,
    How oft! I bless the Lot that made me love you.

—Samuel Taylor Coleridge

26 Song: To Celia

Drink to me only with thine eyes,
    And I will pledge with mine;
Or leave a kiss but in the cup,
    And I'll not look for wine.
The thirst that from the soul doth rise
    Doth ask a drink divine:
But might I of Jove's nectar sup,
    I would not change for thine.
I sent thee a rosy wreath,
    Not so much honouring thee,
As giving it a hope that there
    It could not withered be.
But thou thereon didst only breathe,
    And sent'st it back to me:
Since when it grows, and smells, I swear,
    Not of itself, but thee.

    —*Ben Jonson*

27 Bright Star

Bright star! would I were steadfast as thou art—
    Not in lone splendour hung aloft the night
And watching, with eternal lids apart,
    Like nature's patient, sleepless Eremite,
The moving waters at their priestlike task
    Of pure ablution round earth's human shores,
Or gazing on the new soft-fallen mask
    Of snow upon the mountains and the moors—
No—yet still steadfast, still unchangeable,
    Pillow'd upon my fair love's ripening breast,
To feel for ever its soft fall and swell,
    Awake for ever in a sweet unrest,
Still, still to hear her tender-taken breath,
And so live ever—or else swoon to death.
    —*John Keats*

 Two in the Campagna

I
I wonder do you feel to-day
    As I have felt since, hand in hand,
We sat down on the grass, to stray
    In spirit better through the land,
This morn of Rome and May?

II
For me, I touched a thought, I know,
    Has tantalized me many times,
(Like turns of thread the spiders throw
    Mocking across our path) for rhymes
To catch at and let go.

III
Help me to hold it! First it left
    The yellowing fennel, run to seed
There, branching from the brickwork's cleft,
    Some old tomb's ruin: yonder weed
Took up the floating weft,

IV

Where one small orange cup amassed
    Five beetles,—blind and green they grope
Among the honey-meal: and last,
    Everywhere on the grassy slope
I traced it. Hold it fast!

V

The champaign with its endless fleece
    Of feathery grasses everywhere!
Silence and passion, joy and peace,
    An everlasting wash of air—
Rome's ghost since her decease.

VI

Such life here, through such lengths of hours,
    Such miracles performed in play,
Such primal naked forms of flowers,
    Such letting nature have her way
While heaven looks from its towers!

VII

How say you? Let us, O my dove,
    Let us be unashamed of soul,
As earth lies bare to heaven above!
    How is it under our control
To love or not to love?

VIII

I would that you were all to me,
    You that are just so much, no more.
Nor yours nor mine, nor slave nor free!
    Where does the fault lie? What the core
O' the wound, since wound must be?

IX

I would I could adopt your will,
    See with your eyes, and set my heart
Beating by yours, and drink my fill
    At your soul's springs,—your part my part
In life, for good and ill.

X

No. I yearn upward, touch you close,
    Then stand away. I kiss your cheek,
Catch your soul's warmth,—I pluck the rose
    And love it more than tongue can speak—
Then the good minute goes.

XI

Already how am I so far
    Out of that minute? Must I go
Still like the thistle-ball, no bar,
    Onward, whenever light winds blow,
Fixed by no friendly star?

XII
Just when I seemed about to learn!
 Where is the thread now? Off again!
The old trick! Only I discern—
 Infinite passion, and the pain
Of finite hearts that yearn.
 —*Robert Browning*

 **Eros**

The sense of the world is short,—
Long and various the report,—
 To love and be beloved;
Men and gods have not outlearned it;
And, how oft soe'er they've turned it,
 'Tis not to be improved.
 —*Ralph Waldo Emerson*

30 The Owl and the Pussy-Cat

I
The Owl and the Pussy-Cat went to sea
    In a beautiful pea-green boat:
They took some honey, and plenty of money
    Wrapped up in a five-pound note.
The Owl looked up to the stars above,
    And sang to a small guitar,
"O lovely Pussy, O Pussy, my love,
    What a beautiful Pussy you are,
        You are,
        You are!
    What a beautiful Pussy you are!"

II
Pussy said to the Owl, "You elegant fowl,
    How charmingly sweet you sing!
Oh! let us be married; too long we have tarried,
    But what shall we do for a ring?"
They sailed away, for a year and a day,
    To the land where the bong-tree grows;
And there in a wood a Piggy-wig stood,
    With a ring at the end of his nose,
        His nose,
        His nose,
    With a ring at the end of his nose.

III
"Dear Pig, are you willing to sell for one shilling
    Your ring?" Said the Piggy, "I will."
So they took it away, and were married next day
    By the Turkey who lives on the hill.
They dined on mince and slices of quince,
    Which they ate with a runcible spoon;
And hand in hand, on the edge of the sand,
    They danced by the light of the moon,
        The moon,
        The moon,
    They danced by the light of the moon.
    —Edward Lear

31) Love and Harmony

Love and harmony combine,
And round our souls entwine
While thy branches mix with mine,
And our roots together join.

Joys upon our branches sit,
Chirping loud and singing sweet;
Like gentle streams beneath our feet
Innocence and virtue meet.

Thou the golden fruit dost bear,
I am clad in flowers fair;
Thy sweet boughs perfume the air,
And the turtle buildeth there.

There she sits and feeds her young,
Sweet I hear her mournful song;
And thy lovely leaves among,
There is love, I hear his tongue.

There his charming nest doth lay,
There he sleeps the night away;
There he sports along the day,
And doth among our branches play.
—*William Blake*

32 If You Were Coming in the Fall

If you were coming in the Fall,
I'd brush the Summer by
With half a smile and half a spurn,
As Housewives do a Fly.

If I could see you in a year,
I'd wind the months in balls—
And put them each in separate Drawers,
For fear the numbers fuse—

If only Centuries, delayed,
I'd count them on my Hand,
Subtracting, till my fingers dropped
Into Van Diemen's Land.

If certain, when this life was out—
That yours and mine, should be,
I'd toss it yonder, like a Rind,
And take Eternity—

But, now, uncertain of the length
Of this, that is between,
It goads me, like the Goblin Bee
That will not state its sting.

—*Emily Dickinson*

33) Remember

Remember me when I am gone away,
  Gone far away into the silent land;
  When you can no more hold me by the hand,
Nor I half turn to go, yet turning stay.
Remember me when no more day by day
  You tell me of our future that you plann'd:
  Only remember me; you understand
It will be late to counsel then or pray.
Yet if you should forget me for a while
  And afterwards remember, do not grieve:
  For if the darkness and corruption leave
A vestige of the thoughts that once I had,
Better by far you should forget and smile
  Than that you should remember and be sad.
  —*Christina Rossetti*

34 Sonnet 154

The little Love-god lying once asleep,
Laid by his side his heart-inflaming brand,
Whilst many nymphs that vow'd chaste life to keep
Came tripping by; but in her maiden hand
The fairest votary took up that fire
Which many legions of true hearts had warm'd;
And so the general of hot desire
Was, sleeping, by a virgin hand disarm'd.
This brand she quenched in a cool well by,
Which from Love's fire took heat perpetual,
Growing a bath and healthful remedy,
For men diseas'd: but I, my mistress' thrall,
    Came there for cure and this by that I prove,
    Love's fire heats water, water cools not love.

—William Shakespeare

35 Meet Me in the Green Glen

Love, meet me in the green glen,
    Beside the tall elm-tree,
Where the sweetbriar smells so sweet agen;
    There come with me.
        Meet me in the green glen.

Meet me at the sunset
    Down in the green glen,
Where we've often met
    By hawthorn-tree and foxes' den,
        Meet me in the green glen.

Meet me in the green glen,
    By sweetbriar bushes there;
Meet me by your own sen,
    Where the wild thyme blossoms fair.
        Meet me in the green glen.

Meet me by the sweetbriar,
    By the mole-hill swelling there;
When the west glows like a fire
    God's crimson bed is there.
        Meet me in the green glen.
    —*John Clare*

36 I Am Not Yours

I am not yours, not lost in you,
    Not lost, altho' I long to be
Lost as a candle lit at noon,
    Lost as a snow-flake in the sea.

You love me, and I find you still
    A spirit beautiful and bright,
Yet I am I, who long to be
    Lost as a light is lost in light.

Oh plunge me deep in love—put out
    My senses, leave me deaf and blind,
Swept by the tempest of your love,
    A taper in a rushing wind.
    —*Sara Teasdale*

37 All for Love

O talk not to me of a name great in story;
The days of our youth are the days of our glory;
And the myrtle and ivy of sweet two-and-twenty
Are worth all your laurels, though ever so plenty.

What are garlands and crowns to the brow that is
    wrinkled?
'Tis but as a dead flower with May-dew besprinkled:
Then away with all such from the head that is hoary—
What care I for the wreaths that can *only* give glory?

O Fame!—if I e'er took delight in thy praises,
'Twas less for the sake of thy high-sounding phrases,
Than to see the bright eyes of the dear one discover
She thought that I was not unworthy to love her.

There chiefly I sought thee, *there* only I found thee;
Her glance was the best of the rays that surround thee;
When it sparkled o'er aught that was bright in my story,
I knew it was love, and I felt it was glory.
    —Lord Byron

38) A Red, Red Rose

O my Luve's like a red, red rose
That's newly sprung in June:
O my Luve's like the melodie
That's sweetly play'd in tune!

As fair art thou, my bonnie lass,
So deep in luve am I:
And I will luve thee still, my dear,
Till a' the seas gang dry:

Till a' the seas gang dry, my dear,
And the rocks melt wi' the sun;
I will luve thee still, my dear,
While the sands o' life shall run.

And fare-thee-weel, my only Luve,
And fare-thee-weel a while!
And I will come again, my Luve,
Tho' it were ten thousand mile.
—*Robert Burns*

39 It's All I Have to Bring Today

It's all I have to bring today—
This, and my heart beside—
This, and my heart, and all the fields—
And all the meadows wide—
Be sure you count—should I forget
Some one the sum could tell—
This, and my heart, and all the Bees
Which in the Clover dwell.
    —*Emily Dickinson*

40 Sonnet 18

Shall I compare thee to a summer's day?
Thou art more lovely and more temperate:
Rough winds do shake the darling buds of May,
And summer's lease hath all too short a date;
Sometime too hot the eye of heaven shines,
And often is his gold complexion dimm'd;
And every fair from fair sometime declines,
By chance, or nature's changing course, untrimm'd.
But thy eternal summer shall not fade,
Nor lose possession of that fair thou owest;
Nor shall Death brag thou wanderest in his shade,
When in eternal lines to time thou growest:—
    So long as men can breathe, or eyes can see,
    So long lives this, and this gives life to thee.
    —*William Shakespeare*

41 Secret Love

I hid my love when young till I
Couldn't bear the buzzing of a fly;
I hid my love to my despite
Till I could not bear to look at light:
I dare not gaze upon her face
But left her memory in each place;

Where'er I saw a wild flower lie
I kissed and bade my love good-bye.

I met her in the greenest dells
Where dewdrops pearl the wood blue bells
The lost breeze kissed her bright blue eye,
The bee kissed and went singing by,
A sunbeam found a passage there,
A gold chain round her neck so fair;
As secret as the wild bee's song
She lay there all the summer long.

I hid my love in field and town
Till e'en the breeze would knock me down,
The bees seemed singing ballads oer,
The fly's bass turned a lion's roar;
And even silence found a tongue,
To haunt me all the summer long;
The riddle nature could not prove
Was nothing else but secret love.
    —John Clare

42   From the Arabic: An Imitation

I
My faint spirit was sitting in the light
Of thy looks, my love;
It panted for thee like the hind at noon
For the brooks, my love.
Thy barb, whose hoofs outspeed the tempest's flight,
Bore thee far from me;
My heart, for my weak feet were weary soon,
Did companion thee.

II
Ah! fleeter far than fleetest storm or steed,
Or the death they bear,
The heart which tender thought clothes like a dove
With the wings of care;
In the battle, in the darkness, in the need,
Shall mine cling to thee,
Nor claim one smile for all the comfort, love,
It may bring to thee.
    —*Percy Bysshe Shelley*

43. A Decade

When you came, you were like red wine and honey,
And the taste of you burnt my mouth with its sweetness
Now you are like morning bread,
Smooth and pleasant.
I hardly taste you at all for I know your savour,
But I am completely nourished.
 —Amy Lowell

44 Sweet-and-Twenty

O mistress mine, where are you roaming?
O stay and hear! your true-love's coming
    That can sing both high and low;
Trip no further, pretty sweeting,
Journey's end in lovers' meeting—
    Every wise man's son doth know.

What is love? 'tis not hereafter;
Present mirth hath present laughter;
    What's to come is still unsure:
In delay there lies no plenty,—
Then come kiss me, Sweet and twenty,
    Youth's a stuff will not endure.
    —*William Shakespeare*

45 Sonnet 33

Yes, call me by my pet-name! let me hear
The name I used to run at, when a child,
From innocent play, and leave the cowslips plied,
To glance up in some face that proved me dear
With the look of its eyes. I miss the clear
Fond voices which, being drawn and reconciled
Into the music of Heaven's undefiled,
Call me no longer. Silence on the bier,
While I call God—call God!—so let thy mouth
Be heir to those who are now exanimate.
Gather the north flowers to complete the south,
And catch the early love up in the late.
Yes, call me by that name,—and I, in truth,
With the same heart, will answer and not wait.
   —*Elizabeth Barrett Browning*

46 Love Will Find Out the Way

Over the mountains
    And over the waves,
Under the fountains
    And under the graves;
Under floods that are deepest,
    Which Neptune obey,
Over rocks that are steepest,
    Love will find out the way.

When there is no place
    For the glow-worm to lie,
When there is no space
    For receipt of a fly;
When the midge dares not venture
    Lest herself fast as she lay,
If Love come, he will enter
    And will find out the way.

You may esteem him
    A child for his might;
Or you may deem him
    A coward for his flight;
But if she whom Love doth honour
    Be conceal'd from the day—
Set a thousand guards upon her,
    Love will find out the way.

Some think to lose him
    By having him confined;
And some do suppose him,
    Poor heart! to be blind;
But if ne'er so close ye wall him,
    Do the best that ye may,
Blind Love, if so ye call him,
    He will find out his way.

You may train the eagle
    To stoop to your fist;
Or you may inveigle
    The Phoenix of the east;
The lioness, you may move her
    To give over her prey;
But you'll ne'er stop a lover—
    He will find out the way.

If the earth it should part him,
    He would gallop it o'er;
If the seas should o'erthwart him,
    He would swim to the shore;
Should his Love become a swallow,
    Through the air to stray,
Love will lend wings to follow,
    And will find out the way.

There is no striving
    To cross his intent;
There is no contriving
    His plots to prevent;
But if once the message greet him
    That his True Love doth stay,
If Death should come and meet him,
    Love will find out the way!
    —Anonymous, 17th century

47 The Clod and the Pebble

'Love seeketh not itself to please,
'Nor for itself hath any care;
'But for another gives its ease,
'And builds a Heaven in Hell's despair.'

So sang a little Clod of Clay,
Trodden with the cattle's feet:
But a Pebble of the brook
Warbled out these metres meet:

'Love seeketh only Self to please,
To bind another to its delight;
Joys in another's loss of ease,
And builds a Hell in Heaven's despite.'
   —*William Blake*

48 Love

We cannot live, except thus mutually
We alternate, aware or unaware,
The reflex act of life: and when we bear
Our virtue onward most impulsively,
Most full of invocation, and to be
Most instantly compellant, certes, there
We live most life, whoever breathes most air
And counts his dying years by sun and sea.
But when a soul, by choice and conscience, doth
Throw out her full force on another soul,
The conscience and the concentration both
Make mere life, Love. For Life in perfect whole
And aim consummated, is Love in sooth,
As nature's magnet-heat rounds pole with pole.

—*Elizabeth Barrett Browning*

49 The Definition of Love

I

My Love is of a birth as rare
As 'tis for object strange and high:
It was begotten by Despair
Upon Impossibility.

II

Magnanimous Despair alone
Could show me so divine a thing,
Where feeble Hope could ne'er have flown
But vainly flapped its tinsel wing.

III

And yet I quickly might arrive
Where my extended soul is fixt,
But Fate does iron wedges drive,
And always crowds itself betwixt.

IV

For Fate with jealous eye does see
Two perfect loves; nor lets them close:
Their union would her ruin be,
And her tyrannic power depose.

V
And therefore, her decrees of steel
Us as the distant Poles have placed,
(Though Love's whole world on us doth wheel)
Not by themselves to be embraced.

VI
Unless the giddy Heaven fall,
And earth some new convulsion tear;
And, us to join, the world should all
Be cramped into a planisphere.

VII
As lines so loves oblique may well
Themselves in every angle greet:
But ours so truly parallel,
Though infinite can never meet.

VIII
Therefore the Love which us doth bind,
But Fate so enviously debars,
Is the conjunction of the Mind,
And opposition of the Stars.
    —*Andrew Marvell*

50 First Love

I ne'er was struck before that hour
    With love so sudden and so sweet.
Her face it bloomed like a sweet flower
    And stole my heart away complete.
My face turned pale as deadly pale,
    My legs refused to walk away,
And when she looked what could I ail?
    My life and all seemed turned to clay.

And then my blood rushed to my face
    And took my sight away.
The trees and bushes round the place
    Seemed midnight at noonday.
I could not see a single thing,
    Words from my eyes did start;
They spoke as chords do from the string
    And blood burnt round my heart.

Are flowers the winter's choice?
    Is love's bed always snow?
She seemed to hear my silent voice
    And love's appeal to know.
I never saw so sweet a face
    As that I stood before:
My heart has left its dwelling-place
    And can return no more.
    —John Clare

51 Her Voice

The wild bee reels from bough to bough
    With his furry coat and his gauzy wing.
Now in a lily-cup, and now
    Setting a jacinth bell a-swing,
        In his wandering;
Sit closer love: it was here I trow
    I made that vow,

Swore that two lives should be like one
    As long as the sea-gull loved the sea,
As long as the sunflower sought the sun,—
    It shall be, I said, for eternity
        'Twixt you and me!
Dear friend, those times are over and done,
    Love's web is spun.

Look upward where the poplar trees
    Sway and sway in the summer air,
Here in the valley never a breeze
    Scatters the thistledown, but there
        Great winds blow fair
From the mighty murmuring mystical seas,
    And the wave-lashed leas.

Look upward where the white gull screams,
    What does it see that we do not see?
Is that a star? or the lamp that gleams
    On some outward voyaging argosy,—
        Ah! can it be
We have lived our lives in a land of dreams!
    How sad it seems.

Sweet, there is nothing left to say
    But this, that love is never lost,
Keen winter stabs the breasts of May
    Whose crimson roses burst his frost,
        Ships tempest-tossed
Will find a harbour in some bay,
    And so we may.

And there is nothing left to do
    But to kiss once again, and part,
Nay, there is nothing we should rue,
    I have my beauty,—you your Art,
        Nay, do not start,
One world was not enough for two
    Like me and you.
    —*Oscar Wilde*

52 Sonnet 21

Say over again, and yet once over again,
That thou dost love me,
Though the word repeated
Should seem a "cuckoo-song," as thou dost treat it,
Remember, never to the hill or plain,
Valley and wood, without her cuckoo-strain
Comes the fresh Spring in all her green completed.
Belovèd, I, amid the darkness greeted
By a doubtful spirit-voice, in that doubt's pain
Cry, "Speak once more—thou lovest!" Who can fear
Too many stars, though each in heaven shall roll,
Too many flowers, though each shall crown the year?
Say thou dost love me, love me, love me—toll
The silver iterance!—only minding, Dear,
To love me also in silence with thy soul.
   —*Elizabeth Barrett Browning*

53) Echo

Come to me in the silence of the night;
    Come in the speaking silence of a dream;
Come with soft rounded cheeks and eyes as bright
    As sunlight on a stream;
        Come back in tears,
O memory of hope, love of finished years.

Oh dream how sweet, too sweet, too bitter sweet,
    Whose waking should have been in Paradise,
Where souls brimfull of love abide and meet;
    Where thirsting longing eyes
        Watch the slow door
That opening, letting in, lets out no more.

Yet come to me in dreams, that I may live
    My life again tho' cold in death:
Come back to me in dreams, that I may give
    Pulse for pulse, breath for breath:
        Speak low, lean low,
As long ago, my love, how long ago.
    —*Christina Rossetti*

Sonnet 40

Take all my loves, my love, yea, take them all;
What hast thou then more than thou hadst before?
No love, my love, that thou mayst true love call;
All mine was thine before thou hadst this more.
Then if for my love thou my love receivest,
I cannot blame thee for my love thou usest;
But yet be blamed, if thou thyself deceivest
By wilful taste of what thyself refusest.
I do forgive thy robbery, gentle thief,
Although thou steal thee all my poverty;
And yet, love knows, it is a greater grief
To bear love's wrong than hate's known injury.
    Lascivious grace, in whom all ill well shows,
    Kill me with spites; yet we must not be foes.
  —*William Shakespeare*

55 The White Rose

The red rose whispers of passion,
    And the white rose breathes of love;
O, the red rose is a falcon,
    And the white rose is a dove.

But I send you a cream-white rosebud
    With a flush on its petal tips;
For the love that is purest and sweetest
    Has a kiss of desire on the lips.
    —*John Boyle O'Reilly*

56 Central Park at Dusk

Buildings above the leafless trees
    Loom high as castles in a dream,
While one by one the lamps come out
    To thread the twilight with a gleam.

There is no sign of leaf or bud,
    A hush is over everything—
Silent as women wait for love,
    The world is waiting for the spring.
    —*Sara Teasdale*

Sonnet 12

Indeed this very love which is my boast,
And which, when rising up from breast to brow,
Doth crown me with a ruby large enow
To draw men's eyes and prove the inner cost,—
This love even, all my worth, to the uttermost,
I should not love withal, unless that thou
Hadst set me an example, shown me how,
When first thine earnest eyes with mine were crossed,
And love called love. And thus, I cannot speak
Of love even, as a good thing of my own:
Thy soul hath snatched up mine all faint and weak,
And placed it by thee on a golden throne,—
And that I love (O soul, we must be meek!)
Is by thee only, whom I love alone.

—Elizabeth Barrett Browning

58 Love and Death

Shall we, too, rise forgetful from our sleep,
And shall my soul that lies within your hand
Remember nothing, as the blowing sand
Forgets the palm where long blue shadows creep
When winds along the darkened desert sweep?
Or would it still remember, tho' it spanned
A thousand heavens, while the planets fanned
The vacant ether with their voices deep?
Soul of my soul, no word shall be forgot,
Nor yet alone, beloved, shall we see
The desolation of extinguished suns,
Nor fear the void wherethro' our planet runs,
For still together shall we go and not
Fare forth alone to front eternity.

—*Sara Teasdale*

59 In a Boat

See the stars, love,
In the water much clearer and brighter
Than those above us, and whiter,
Like nenuphars.

Star-shadows shine, love,
How many stars in your bowl?
How many shadows in your soul,
Only mine, love, mine?

When I move the oars, love
See how the stars are tossed,
Distorted, the brightest lost.
—So that bright one of yours, love.

The poor waters spill
The stars, waters broken, forsaken!—
The heavens are not shaken, you say, love;
Its stars stand still.

There, did you see
That spark fly up at us; even
Stars are not safe in heaven.
—What of yours, then, love, yours?

What then, love, if soon
Your light be tossed over a wave?
Will you count the darkness a grave,
And swoon, love, swoon?
 —*D. H. Lawrence*

60) Life in a Love

      Escape me?
      Never—
      Beloved!
While I am I, and you are you,
    So long as the world contains us both,
    Me the loving and you the loth,
While the one eludes, must the other pursue.
My life is a fault at last, I fear—
    It seems too much like a fate, indeed!
    Though I do my best I shall scarce succeed.
But what if I fail of my purpose here?
It is but to keep the nerves at strain,
    To dry one's eyes and laugh at a fall,
And baffled, get up to begin again,—
    So the chace takes up one's life, that's all.
While, look but once from your furthest bound,
    At me so deep in the dust and dark,
No sooner the old hope drops to ground
    Than a new one, straight to the selfsame mark,
      I shape me—
      Ever
      Removed!
    —*Robert Browning*

61) Sonnet 35

If I leave all for thee, wilt thou exchange
And be all to me? Shall I never miss
Home-talk and blessing and the common kiss
That comes to each in turn, nor count it strange,
When I look up, to drop on a new range
Of walls and floors, another home than this?
Nay, wilt thou fill that place by me which is
Filled by dead eyes too tender to know change
That's hardest. If to conquer love, has tried,
To conquer grief, tries more, as all things prove,
For grief indeed is love and grief beside.
Alas, I have grieved so I am hard to love.
Yet love me—wilt thou? Open thy heart wide,
And fold within, the wet wings of thy dove.

—*Elizabeth Barrett Browning*

62 Wooing Song

Love is the blossom where there blows
Every thing that lives or grows:
Love doth make the Heav'ns to move,
And the Sun doth burn in love:
Love the strong and weak doth yoke,
And makes the ivy climb the oak,
Under whose shadows lions wild,
Soften'd by love, grow tame and mild:
Love no med'cine can appease,
He burns the fishes in the seas:
Not all the skill his wounds can stench,
Not all the sea his fire can quench.
Love did make the bloody spear
Once a leavy coat to wear,
While in his leaves there shrouded lay
Sweet birds, for love that sing and play
And of all love's joyful flame
I the bud and blossom am.
    Only bend thy knee to me,
    Thy wooing shall thy winning be!

See, see the flowers that below
Now as fresh as morning blow;
And of all the virgin rose
That as bright Aurora shows;
How they all unleavèd die,
Losing their virginity!
Like unto a summer shade,
But now born, and now they fade.
Everything doth pass away;
There is danger in delay:
Come, come, gather then the rose,
Gather it, or it you lose!
All the sand of Tagus' shore
Into my bosom casts his ore:
All the valleys' swimming corn
To my house is yearly borne:
Every grape of every vine
Is gladly bruised to make me wine:
While ten thousand kings, as proud,
To carry up my train have bow'd,
And a world of ladies send me
In my chambers to attend me:
All the stars in Heav'n that shine,
And ten thousand more, are mine:
    Only bend thy knee to me,
    Thy wooing shall thy winning be!
    —*Giles Fletcher*

63 Annabel Lee

It was many and many a year ago,
    In a kingdom by the sea,
That a maiden there lived whom you may know
    By the name of Annabel Lee;
And this maiden she lived with no other thought
    Than to love and be loved by me.

I was a child and *she* was a child,
    In this kingdom by the sea;
But we loved with a love that was more than love-
    I and my Annabel Lee;
With a love that the wingèd seraphs of Heaven
    Coveted her and me.

And this was the reason that, long ago,
    In this kingdom by the sea,
A wind blew out of a cloud, chilling
    My beautiful Annabel Lee;
So that her highborn kinsman came
    And bore her away from me,
To shut her up in a sepulchre
    In this kingdom by the sea.

The angels, not half so happy in Heaven,
    Went envying her and me—
Yes!-that was the reason (as all men know,
    In this kingdom by the sea)
That the wind came out of the cloud by night,
    Chilling and killing my Annabel Lee.

But our love it was stronger by far than the love
    Of those who were older than we—
    Of many far wiser than we—
And neither the angels in heaven above,
    Nor the demons down under the sea,
Can ever dissever my soul from the soul
    Of the beautiful Annabel Lee.

For the moon never beams without bringing me dreams
    Of the beautiful Annabel Lee;
And the stars never rise but I feel the bright eyes
    Of the beautiful Annabel Lee;
And so, all the night-tide, I lie down by the side
Of my darling—my darling—my life and my bride,
    In the sepulchre there by the sea,
    In her tomb by the sounding sea.
    —Edgar Allan Poe

64 Snow Song

Fairy snow, fairy snow,
Blowing, blowing everywhere,
    Would that I
    Too, could fly
Lightly, lightly through the air.

Like a wee, crystal star
I should drift, I should blow
    Near, more near,
    To my dear
Where he comes through the snow.

I should fly to my love
Like a flake in the storm,
    I should die,
    I should die,
On his lips that are warm.
    —Sara Teasdale

65) Sonnet 47

Betwixt mine eye and heart a league is took,
And each doth good turns now unto the other:
When that mine eye is famish'd for a look,
Or heart in love with sighs himself doth smother,
With my love's picture then my eye doth feast
And to the painted banquet bids my heart;
Another time mine eye is my heart's guest
And in his thoughts of love doth share a part:
So, either by thy picture or my love,
Thyself away art resent still with me;
For thou not farther than my thoughts canst move,
And I am still with them and they with thee;
    Or, if they sleep, thy picture in my sight
    Awakes my heart to heart's and eye's delight.
    —*William Shakespeare*

66. Monna Innominata (I Loved You First)

I loved you first: but afterwards your love,
    Outsoaring mine, sang such a loftier song
As drowned the friendly cooings of my dove.
    Which owes the other most? My love was long,
    And yours one moment seemed to wax more strong;
I loved and guessed at you, you construed me
And loved me for what might or might not be—
    Nay, weights and measures do us both a wrong.
For verily love knows not 'mine' or 'thine';
    With separate 'I' and 'thou' free love has done,
        For one is both and both are one in love:
Rich love knows nought of 'thine that is not mine';
    Both have the strength and both the length thereof,
Both of us, of the love which makes us one.

—*Christina Rossetti*

Sonnet 34

With the same heart, I said, I'll answer thee
As those, when thou shalt call me by my name—
Lo, the vain promise! is the same, the same,
Perplexed and ruffled by life's strategy?
When called before, I told how hastily
I dropped my flowers or brake off from a game.
To run and answer with the smile that came
At play last moment, and went on with me
Through my obedience. When I answer now,
I drop a grave thought, break from solitude;
Yet still my heart goes to thee—ponder how—
Not as to a single good, but all my good!
Lay thy hand on it, best one, and allow
That no child's foot could run fast as this blood.

—Elizabeth Barrett Browning

68. Stanzas ["Oh, Come to Me in Dreams, My Love!"]

Oh, come to me in dreams, my love!
    I will not ask a dearer bliss;
Come with the starry beams, my love,
    And press mine eyelids with thy kiss.

'Twas thus, as ancient fables tell,
    Love visited a Grecian maid,
Till she disturbed the sacred spell,
    And woke to find her hopes betrayed.

But gentle sleep shall veil my sight,
    And Psyche's lamp shall darkling be,
When, in the visions of the night,
    Thou dost renew thy vows to me.

Then come to me in dreams, my love,
    I will not ask a dearer bliss;
Come with the starry beams, my love,
    And press mine eyelids with thy kiss.
    —*Mary Wollstonecraft Shelley*

69) Wild Nights—Wild Nights!

Wild Nights—Wild Nights!
Were I with thee
Wild Nights should be
Our luxury!

Futile—the Winds—
To a Heart in port—
Done with the Compass—
Done with the Chart!

Rowing in Eden—
Ah, the Sea!
Might I moor—Tonight—
In Thee!
    —*Emily Dickinson*

70. The Rose and the Bee

If I were a bee and you were a rose,
Would you let me in when the gray wind blows?
Would you hold your petals wide apart,
Would you let me in to find your heart,
    If you were a rose?

"If I were a rose and you were a bee,
You should never go when you came to me,
I should hold my love on my heart at last,
I should close my leaves and keep you fast,
    If you were a bee."
    —*Sara Teasdale*

71 Lovers' Infiniteness

If yet I have not all the love
    Dear, I shall never have it all,
I cannot breathe one other sigh, to move,
    Nor can entreat one other tear to fall.
All my treasure, which should purchase thee,
    Sighs, tears, and oaths, and letters I have spent,
Yet no more can be due to me,
    Than at the bargain made was meant.
If then thy gift of love were partial,
That some to me, some should to others fall,
    Dear, I shall never have thee all.

Or if then thou gavest me all,
    All was but all, which thou hadst then;
But if in thy heart, since, there be or shall
    New love created be, by other men,
Which have their stocks entire, and can in tears,
    In sighs, in oaths, and letters outbid me,
This new love may beget new fears,
    For, this love was not vowed by thee.
And yet it was, thy gift being general,
The ground, thy heart is mine; whatever shall
    Grow there, dear, I should have it all.

Yet I would not have all yet,
    He that hath all can have no more,
And since my love doth every day admit
    New growth, thou shouldst have new rewards in
        store;
Thou canst not every day give me thy heart,
    If thou canst give it, then thou never gav'st it;
Love's riddles are, that though thy heart depart,
    It stays at home, and thou with losing sav'st it:
But we will have a way more liberal,
Than changing hearts, to join them, so we shall
    Be one, and another's all.

    —John Donne

Sonnet 14

If thou must love me, let it be for nought
Except for love's sake only. Do not say,
"I love her for her smile—her look—her way
Of speaking gently,—for a trick of thought
That falls in well with mine, and certes brought
A sense of pleasant ease on such a day"—
For these things in themselves, Belovèd, may
Be changed, or change for thee—and love, so wrought,
May be unwrought so. Neither love me for
Thine own dear pity's wiping my cheeks dry:
A creature might forget to weep, who bore
Thy comfort long, and lose thy love thereby!
But love me for love's sake, that evermore
Thou mayst love on, through love's eternity.
—*Elizabeth Barrett Browning*

73 The Indian Serenade

I

I arise from dreams of thee
In the first sweet sleep of night,
When the winds are breathing low,
And the stars are shining bright
I arise from dreams of thee,
And a spirit in my feet
Hath led me—who knows how?
To thy chamber window, Sweet!

II

The wandering airs they faint
On the dark, the silent stream—
The Champak odours fail
Like sweet thoughts in a dream;
The nightingale's complaint,
It dies upon her heart;—
As I must on thine,
Oh, beloved as thou art!

III
O lift me from the grass!
I die! I faint! I fail!
Let thy love in kisses rain
On my lips and eyelids pale.
My cheek is cold and white, alas!
My heart beats loud and fast;—
Oh! press it to thine own again,
Where it will break at last.

—*Percy Bysshe Shelley*

I Would Live in Your Love

I would live in your love as the sea-grasses live in the sea,
Borne up by each wave as it passes, drawn down by
 each wave that recedes;
I would empty my soul of the dreams that have
 gathered in me,
I would beat with your heart as it beats, I would follow
 your soul as it leads.

—*Sara Teasdale*

75) The Letter

Little cramped words scrawling all over the paper
Like draggled fly's legs,
What can you tell of the flaring moon
Through the oak leaves?
Or of my uncertain window and the bare floor
Spattered with moonlight?
Your silly quirks and twists have nothing in them
Of blossoming hawthorns,
And this paper is dull, crisp, smooth, virgin of loveliness
Beneath my hand.

I am tired, Beloved, of chafing my heart against
The want of you;
Of squeezing it into little inkdrops,
And posting it.
And I scald alone, under the fire
Of the great moon.
    —*Amy Lowell*

76 The Ragged Wood

O hurry where by water among trees
The delicate-stepping stag and his lady sigh,
When they have but looked upon their images,—
O that none ever loved but you and I!

Or have you heard that sliding silver-shoed
Pale silver-proud queen-woman of the sky,
When the sun looked out of his golden hood,—
O that none ever loved but you and I!

O hurry to the ragged wood, for there
I will drive all those lovers out and cry—
O my share of the world, O yellow hair!
No one has ever loved but you and I.
   —*William Butler Yeats*

77 Sonnet 130

My mistress' eyes are nothing like the sun;
Coral is far more red than her lips' red:
If snow be white, why then her breasts are dun;
If hairs be wires, black wires grow on her head.
I have seen roses damask'd, red and white,
But no such roses see I in her cheeks;
And in some perfumes is there more delight
Than in the breath that from my mistress reeks.
I love to hear her speak, yet well I know
That music hath a far more pleasing sound;
I grant I never saw a goddess go;
My mistress, when she walks, treads on the ground:
    And yet by heaven, I think my love as rare,
    As any she belied with false compare.

—William Shakespeare

78 When the Lamp Is Shattered

I
When the lamp is shattered
The light in the dust lies dead—
When the cloud is scattered,
The rainbow's glory is shed.
When the lute is broken,
Sweet tones are remembered not;
When the lips have spoken,
Loved accents are soon forgot.

II
As music and splendour
Survive not the lamp and the lute,
The heart's echoes render
No song when the spirit is mute—
No song but sad dirges,
Like the wind through a ruined cell,
Or the mournful surges
That ring the dead seaman's knell.

III
When hearts have once mingled,
Love first leaves the well-built nest;
The weak one is singled
To endure what it once possessed.
O Love! who bewailest
The frailty of all things here,
Why choose you the frailest
For your cradle, your home, and your bier?

IV
Its passions will rock thee,
As the storms rock the ravens on high;
Bright reason will mock thee,
Like the sun from a wintry sky.
From thy nest every rafter
Will rot, and thine eagle home
Leave thee naked to laughter,
When leaves fall and cold winds come.
  —*Percy Bysshe Shelley*

79 Joy

I am wild, I will sing to the trees,
    I will sing to the stars in the sky,
    I love, I am loved, he is mine,
        Now at last I can die!
I am sandaled with wind and with flame,
    I have heart-fire and singing to give,
    I can tread on the grass or the stars,
        Now at last I can live!

    —*Sara Teasdale*

80 Monna Innominata [I Wish I Could Remember]

I wish I could remember that first day,
    First hour, first moment of your meeting me,
    If bright or dim the season, it might be
Summer or Winter for aught I can say;
So unrecorded did it slip away,
    So blind was I to see and to foresee,
    So dull to mark the budding of my tree
That would not blossom for many a May.
If only I could recollect it, such
    A day of days! I let it come and go
    As traceless as a thaw of bygone snow;
It seemed to mean so little, meant so much;
If only now I could recall that touch,
    First touch of hand in hand—Did one but know!
    —*Christina Rossetti*

81 A Love Song

Reject me not if I should say to you
I do forget the sounding of your voice,
I do forget your eyes, that searching through
The mists perceive our marriage, and rejoice.

Yet, when the apple-blossom opens wide
Under the pallid moonlight's fingering,
I see your blanched face at my breast, and hide
My eyes from diligent work, malingering.

Ah, then upon my bedroom I do draw
The blind to hide the garden, where the moon
Enjoys the open blossoms as they straw
Their beauty for his taking, boon for boon.

And I do lift my aching arms to you,
And I do lift my anguished, avid breast,
And I do weep for very pain of you,
And fling myself at the doors of sleep, for rest.

And I do toss through the troubled night for you,
Dreaming your yielded mouth is given to mine,
Feeling your strong breast carry me on into
The peace where sleep is stronger even than wine.
    —*D. H. Lawrence*

82 Spring Night

The park is filled with night and fog,
    The veils are drawn about the world,
        The drowsy lights along the paths
           Are dim and pearled.

Gold and gleaming the empty streets,
Gold and gleaming the misty lake,
    The mirrored lights like sunken swords,
        Glimmer and shake.

    Oh, is it not enough to be
Here with this beauty over me?
My throat should ache with praise, and I
    Should kneel in joy beneath the sky.
    O beauty, are you not enough?
Why am I crying after love,
With youth, a singing voice, and eyes
    To take earth's wonder with surprise?
Why have I put off my pride,
    Why am I unsatisfied,—
I, for whom the pensive night

Binds her cloudy hair with light,—
    I, for whom all beauty burns
    Like incense in a million urns?
    O beauty, are you not enough?
    Why am I crying after love?
    —*Sara Teasdale*

83) The Passionate Shepherd to His Love

Come live with me and be my love,
And we will all the pleasures prove
That valleys, groves, hills, and fields,
Woods or steepy mountain yields.

And we will sit upon the rocks,
Seeing the shepherds feed their flocks,
By shallow rivers to whose falls
Melodious birds sing madrigals.

And I will make thee beds of roses
And a thousand fragrant posies,
A cap of flowers, and a kirtle
Embroidered all with leaves of myrtle;

A gown made of the finest wool
Which from our pretty lambs we pull;
Fair lined slippers for the cold,
With buckles of the purest gold;

A belt of straw and ivy buds,
With coral clasps and amber studs:
And if these pleasures may thee move,
Come live with me and be my love.

The shepherds' swains shall dance and sing
For thy delight each May morning:
If these delights thy mind may move,
Then live with me and be my love.
—*Christopher Marlowe*

84 Sonnet 10

Yet, love, mere love, is beautiful indeed
And worthy of acceptation. Fire is bright,
Let temple burn, or flax; an equal light
Leaps in the flame from cedar-plank or weed:
And love is fire. And when I say at need
I love thee . . . mark!. . . I love thee—in thy sight
I stand transfigured, glorified aright,
With conscience of the new rays that proceed
Out of my face toward thine. There's nothing low
In love, when love the lowest: meanest creatures
Who love God, God accepts while loving so.
And what I feel, across the inferior features
Of what I am, doth flash itself, and show
How that great work of Love enhances Nature's.

—*Elizabeth Barrett Browning*

85 Good-Night

I

Good-night? ah! no; the hour is ill
Which severs those it should unite;
Let us remain together still,
Then it will be *good* night.

II

How can I call the lone night good,
Though thy sweet wishes wing its flight?
Be it not said, thought, understood—
Then it will be—*good* night.

III

To hearts which near each other move
From evening close to morning light,
The night is good; because, my love,
They never *say* good-night.

—*Percy Bysshe Shelley*

86 Romance

I will make you brooches and toys for your delight
Of bird-song at morning and star-shine at night.
I will make a palace fit for you and me,
Of green days in forests and blue days at sea.

I will make my kitchen, and you shall keep your room,
Where white flows the river and bright blows the broom,
And you shall wash your linen and keep your body white
In rainfall at morning and dewfall at night.

And this shall be for music when no else is near,
The fine song for singing, the rare song to hear!
That only I remember, that only you admire,
Of the broad road that stretches and the roadside fire.

—*Robert Louis Stevenson*

87) Peace

Peace flows into me
    As the tide to the pool by the shore;
    It is mine forevermore,
It ebbs not back like the sea.

I am the pool of blue
    That worships the vivid sky;
    My hopes were heaven-high,
They are all fulfilled in you.

I am the pool of gold
    When sunset burns and dies,—
    You are my deepening skies,
Give me your stars to hold.
    —*Sara Teasdale*

88. Down by the Salley Gardens

Down by the salley gardens my love and I did meet;
She passed the salley gardens with little snow-white feet.
She bid me take love easy, as the leaves grow on the tree;
But I, being young and foolish, with her would not agree.

In a field by the river my love and I did stand,
And on my leaning shoulder she laid her snow-white
    hand.
She bid me take life easy, as the grass grows on the weirs;
But I was young and foolish, and now am full of tears.

—*William Butler Yeats*

89. Opal

You are ice and fire,
The touch of you burns my hands like snow.
You are cold and flame.
You are the crimson of amaryllis,
The silver of moon-touched magnolias.
When I am with you,
My heart is a frozen pond
Gleaming with agitated torches.

—*Amy Lowell*

90 Surrender

Doubt Me! My Dim Companion!
Why, God, would be content
With but a fraction of the Life—
Poured thee without a stint—
The whole of me—forever—
What more the Woman can,—
Say quick, that I may dower thee
With last Delight I own!

It cannot be my Spirit,
For that was thine, before—
I ceded all of dust I knew—
What Opulence the more
Had I, a freckled Maiden,
Whose farthest of degree,
Was—that she might—
Some distant Heaven,
Dwell timidly, with thee!
  —*Emily Dickinson*

91 A Complaint

There is a change—and I am poor;
Your love hath been, nor long ago,
A Fountain at my fond Heart's door,
Whose only business was to flow;
And flow it did; not taking heed
Of its own bounty, or my need.

What happy moments did I count!
Blest was I then all bliss above!
Now, for that consecrated fount
Of murmuring, sparkling, living love,
What have I? shall I dare to tell?
A comfortless and hidden well.

A Well of love—it may be deep—
I trust it is,—and never dry:
What matter? if the Waters sleep
In silence and obscurity.
—Such change, and at the very door
Of my fond Heart, hath made me poor.

   —William Wordsworth

92 Meeting at Night

The gray sea and the long black land;
And the yellow half-moon large and low;
And the startled little waves that leap
In fiery ringlets from their sleep,
As I gain the cove with pushing prow,
And quench its speed i' the slushy sand.

Then a mile of warm sea-scented beach;
Three fields to cross till a farm appears;
A tap at the pane, the quick sharp scratch
And blue spurt of a lighted match,
And a voice less loud, through its joys and fears,
Than the two hearts beating each to each!
   —*Robert Browning*

93 Sonnet 137

Thou blind fool, Love, what dost thou to mine eyes,
That they behold, and see not what they see?
They know what beauty is, see where it lies,
Yet what the best is take the worst to be.
If eyes, corrupt by over-partial looks,
Be anchor'd in the bay where all men ride,
Why of eyes' falsehood hast thou forged hooks,
Whereto the judgment of my heart is tied?
Why should my heart think that a several plot,
Which my heart knows the wide world's common place?
Or mine eyes, seeing this, say this is not,
To put fair truth upon so foul a face?
    In things right true my heart and eyes have err'd,
    And to this false plague are they now transferr'd.
    —*William Shakespeare*

94. The Genesis of Butterflies

The dawn is smiling on the dew that covers
The tearful roses; lo, the little lovers
That kiss the buds, and all the flutterings
In jasmine bloom, and privet, of white wings,
That go and come, and fly, and peep and hide,
With muffled music, murmured far and wide!
Ah, Spring time, when we think of all the lays
That dreamy lovers send to dreamy mays,
Of the fond hearts within a billet bound,
Of all the soft silk paper that pens wound,
The messages of love that mortals write
Filled with intoxication of delight,
Written in April, and before the May time
Shredded and flown, play things for the wind's play-time,
We dream that all white butterflies above,
Who seek through clouds or waters souls to love,
And leave their lady mistress in despair,
To flit to flowers, as kinder and more fair,
Are but torn love-letters, that through the skies
Flutter, and float, and change to butterflies.

—*Victor Hugo*

95 Corinne's Last Love Song

I

How beautiful, how beautiful you streamed upon my sight,
In glory and in grandeur, as a gorgeous sunset-light!
How softly, soul-subduing, fell your words upon mine ear,
Like low aerial music when some angel hovers near!
What tremulous, faint ecstasy to clasp your hand in mine,
Till the darkness fell upon me of a glory too divine!
The air around grew languid with our intermingled breath,
And in your beauty's shadow I sank motionless as death.
I saw you not, I heard not, for a mist was on my brain—
I only felt that life could give no joy like that again.

II

And this was Love, I knew it not, but blindly floated on,
And now I'm on the ocean waste, dark, desolate, alone;
The waves are raging round me—I'm reckless where they guide;
No hope is left to right me, no strength to stem the tide.
As a leaf along the torrent, a cloud across the sky,
As dust upon the whirlwind, so my life is drifting by.
The dream that drank the meteor's light—the form from
    Heav'n has flown—
The vision and the glory, they are passing—they are gone.
Oh! love is frantic agony, and life one throb of pain;
Yet I would bear its darkest woes to dream that dream again.

    —*Lady Jane Wilde*

96 Leave Me, O Love, Which Reachest but to Dust

Leave me, O Love, which reachest but to dust,
And thou my mind aspire to higher things:
Grow rich in that which never taketh rust:
Whatever fades, but fading pleasure brings.

Draw in thy beams, and humble all thy might,
To that sweet yoke, where lasting freedoms be:
Which breaks the clouds and opens forth the light,
That both doth shine and give us sight to see.

O take fast hold, let that light be thy guide,
In this small course which birth draws out to death,
And think how evil becometh him to slide,
Who seeketh heaven, and comes of heavenly breath.

Then farewell world, thy uttermost I see,
Eternal Love, maintain thy life in me.

—*Sir Philip Sidney*

97 Sonnet 22

When our two souls stand up erect and strong,
Face to face, silent, drawing nigh and nigher,
Until the lengthening wings break into fire
At either curvèd point,—what bitter wrong
Can the earth do to us, that we should not long
Be here contented? Think! In mounting higher,
The angels would press on us and aspire
To drop some golden orb of perfect song
Into our deep, dear silence. Let us stay
Rather on earth, Belovèd,—where the unfit
Contrarious moods of men recoil away
And isolate pure spirits, and permit
A place to stand and love in for a day,
With darkness and the death-hour rounding it.

—*Elizabeth Barrett Browning*

98 Music, When Soft Voices Die

Music, when soft voices die,
Vibrates in the memory—
Odours, when sweet violets sicken,
Live within the sense they quicken.

Rose leaves, when the rose is dead,
Are heap'd for the belovèd's bed;
And so thy thoughts, when thou art gone,
Love itself shall slumber on.
    —*Percy Bysshe Shelley*

 99 Less Than the Cloud to the Wind

Less than the cloud to the wind,
    Less than the foam to the sea,
Less than the rose to the storm
    Am I to thee.

More than the star to the night,
    More than the rain to the lea,
More than heaven to earth
    Art thou to me.
    —*Sara Teasdale*

100) The Lily

The modest Rose puts forth a thorn,
The humble sheep a threat'ning horn:
While the Lily white shall in love delight,
Nor a thorn nor a threat stain her beauty bright.
　　—*William Blake*

author index

Anonymous, 17th century   52
Barrett Browning, Elizabeth   5, 14, 51, 56, 63, 67, 72, 80, 86, 101, 113
Best, Charles   19
Blake, William   37, 55, 115
Bradstreet, Anne   20
Brennan, Christopher John   12
Browning, Robert   2, 31, 71, 108
Burns, Robert   44
Byron, Lord   23, 43
Clare, John   24, 41, 46, 59
Coleridge, Samuel Taylor   28
Dickinson, Emily   3, 27, 38, 45, 82, 106
Donne, John   84
Emerson, Ralph Waldo   34
Fletcher, Giles   73
Hugo, Victor   9, 110
Jonson, Ben   29
Keats, John   30
Lawrence, D. H.   17, 69, 96
Lear, Edward   35
Lowell, Amy   49, 89, 105

Marlowe, Christopher   99
Marvell, Andrew   57
O'Reilly, John Boyle   66
Petrarch   7
Poe, Edgar Allan   75
Rossetti, Christina   10, 39, 64, 79, 95
Shakespeare, William   1, 11, 22, 40, 46, 50, 65, 78, 91, 109
Shelley, Mary Wollstonecraft   81
Shelley, Percy Bysshe   13, 48, 87, 92, 102, 114
Sidney, Sir Philip   112
Spenser, Edmund   4
Stevenson, Robert Louis   103
Teasdale, Sara   8, 26, 42, 66, 68, 77, 83, 88, 94, 98, 104, 114
Tennyson, Alfred, Lord   15
Wilde, Lady Jane   111
Wilde, Oscar   61
Wordsworth, William   21, 107
Yeats, William Butler   6, 90, 105

COLLECT ALL TITLES IN THE POCKET POSH® SERIES!

Complete Calorie Counter
Word Power: 120 Words You Should Know
Word Power: 120 Words to Make You Sound Intelligent
Word Power: 120 Job Interview Words You Should Know
Word Power: 120 Words That Are Fun to Say
Dining Out Calorie Counter
Cocktails
Tips for Quilters
Tips for Knitters
Guide to Great Home Video
Tips for Travelers
Wine
Tips for Bridge Players
Tips for Poker Players
Sewing Tips
100 Classic Love Poems
100 Classic Poems
Puzzle Series